pader

Vägg

KH

FAL

PARED

NOMOCINIW

ఓ సొ అొ
cc

Wand

परकाल

UKURI

KIBAKA

MUR

SCIANA

ᚦᛟᛗᛒᛟᚲ

Do you know about other walls? Are they visible or invisible? Are they monuments? Do they tell stories? How are walls built? Do they need to stay up or come down? Do you build walls? Would you tear them down? Can you imagine a world without walls?

墙

12 The Vietnam Veterans Memorial

Jan Scruggs, a Vietnam War veteran, vowed in 1979 that a memorial would be built with the names of all Americans dead and missing as a result of the war. After political support from Congress and many private donations were obtained, a competition was held to choose the design. Maya Lin's design was chosen over 1,400 other entries. Construction was completed for dedication on November 11, 1982.

The 493.5-foot wall has 58,156 American names chiseled into it. At least 2,150,000 Vietnamese, 200,000 Cambodians, and 100,000 Laotians were also killed during the conflict, which lasted from the late 1950s to 1975.

A giant step is about three feet long.

13 Nelson Mandela's Prison Walls

Nelson Mandela has been one of many political prisoners worldwide. Martin Luther King, Mohandas K. Gandhi, Henry David Thoreau, Stephen Biko, and countless others have been imprisoned because they have spoken out against their governments. Aung San Suu Kyi received the 1991 Nobel Peace Prize, even though at that time she was a political prisoner under house arrest in Myanmar (formerly Burma).

Mandela spent time in two South African prisons, Robben Island and Pollsmoor. For fourteen years he wasn't allowed any contact with his family, and he was often denied his books. In June 1991, apartheid laws of legal segregation were repealed in South Africa.

14 The Berlin Wall

In August of 1961, construction of the Berlin Wall began under the direction of Nikita Khrushchev, leader of the Soviet Union. The wall physically sealed off West Berlin from East Berlin and stopped all traffic between the two cities.

There were no solid barriers along the borders of the Iron Curtain countries (Albania, Romania, Czechoslovakia, Poland, the Soviet Union, Bulgaria, Hungary, and East Germany) but in some places barbed wire was erected and land mines planted.

Since the Berlin Wall was torn down, many changes have taken place. East and West Germany have united as one country, and the city of Berlin will once again be the capital of a united Germany.

Endpapers

Written on the endpapers is the word for wall in these thirty-six languages: Shona, Kikongo, Tagalog, Korean, Hindi, Polish, Dutch, Hungarian, Russian, Arabic, Vietnamese, Portuguese, Esperanto, Italian, Swedish, Greek, Hebrew, Rumanian, Czech, Passamaquoddy, Swahili, Sinhalese, Nepali, Papago-Pima, French, Yiddish, Chinese, Kikuyu, German, Khmer, Spanish, Serbo-Croatian, Turkish, Indonesian, Danish, and English.

How This Book Came To Be Written

Doug Rawlings is a poet, writing instructor, and co-founder of Veterans for Peace, Inc. His poems–particularly one with the lines "I kneel / staring into the Wall / through my own reflection / beyond the names of those who died so young"–were the inspiration for *Talking Walls*.

9 The Taos Pueblo

Pueblos are permanent adobe homes. The Tiwa people live at the Taos pueblo and call their home "Red Willow Place." The original architecture has remained the same, though over the years doors and windows have been added. In 1970, after many decades of dispute, the U.S. government returned fifty thousand acres of land surrounding the pueblo to the Tiwa.

Pueblo is the Spanish word for "village." There are many active pueblos in the United States, primarily in Arizona and New Mexico.

At the Acoma pueblo in New Mexico, the inhabitants of one of the oldest settlements in the country, the Keres people, live on top of a 357-foot-high mesa.

10 Mexican Murals

For thousands of years murals have been painted on walls throughout the world. Diego Rivera, José Orozco, and David Siquerois were the major Mexican artists who revived mural painting in Mexico in the 1930s. Rivera lived from 1886 to 1957. Although he was a controversial artist in Mexico, he was instrumental in a successful campaign to allow Mexican artists to paint the walls of government buildings.

During the Great Depression, Rivera was hired to paint a mural in New York City's Rockefeller Center. But when the people who commissioned him saw the painting they objected to its political content. When Rivera refused to change it, they had it destroyed. E. B. White wrote a ballad about this mural with the refrain "'I paint what I paint, I paint what I see, I paint what I think,' said Rivera. . . ."

11 The Canadian Museum of Civilization

Douglas Cardinal's grandmother was a Canadian Blackfoot. Cardinal designed his visual image of the Canadian Museum of Civilization while sitting with friends in a sweat lodge in Stony Plain, Canada. He presented his designs to the Canadian government more than eighty times before they finally gave approval and funding for the museum in 1983.

A friend who had been with Cardinal in the sweat lodge traveled to Hull when the museum was being constructed and remarked how similar it was to Cardinal's vision that day in Stony Plain. The museum, which opened in June of 1989, was built with limestone from Manitoba.

5 Mahabalipuram's Animal Walls

The carved animals on the rock wall in Mahabalipuram are part of the world's longest bas-relief. Today in Mahabalipuram, artists from its sculptor school keep busy repairing these carvings and Indian temples.

The diverse people of India have loved and revered animals for a long time. Buddhists, Hindus, and Jains regard all forms of life as important and believe that when a creature dies it comes back in another form. Animals have also been an important feature of Muslim art in India.

6 Muslim Walls

The pilgrimage to Mecca is the fifth pillar of the Muslim faith and the only nonmandatory one. Muslims are asked to believe in Allah, their God. Many Muslims pray five times a day facing Mecca, donate part of their income to the needy, fast during Ramadhan (a month of Thanksgiving), and, if they are financially and physically able, make one trip to Mecca.

After visiting the Ka'aba, Muslims continue their pilgrimage by journeying to other holy areas near Mecca where they pray and complete their rituals.

7 Great Zimbabwe

Today, the country of Zimbabwe proudly displays a green bird on its flag. Many of these birds, carved from soapstone, once perched on the walls of Great Zimbabwe, a city that served as a political and trade center during the fourteenth and fifteenth centuries. The rediscovery of the walls in 1867 resulted in great damage to them because people had heard that gold had been hidden in them. Today these walls are historical ruins.

8 Cuzco, Peru

Cuzco was founded in the eleventh century and was once the capital of the vast Inca empire. Often called the "City of the Sun," it is well known for its archaeological ruins. The stones used to build the walls around the city were transported long distances by workers using levers.

In 1533 the Spanish, led by Pizarro, took Cuzco and stole much of the gold off the Incas' walls. Spaniards later built the Church of Santo Domingo on top of the old foundation of the Incas' Temple of the Sun. The church has crumbled twice due to earthquakes, but the Inca walls have remained intact.

1 The Great Wall of China

About twenty-five hundred years ago millions of workers began to build this thirty-foot-high wall entirely by hand. The wall is sometimes called the longest cemetery in the world because thousands of workers died due to the harsh conditions under which they were forced to labor. Around 214 B.C. many sections of the wall were connected for the first time. During the last two hundred years the Great Wall has been repaired many times.

In 135 A.D., a similar protective wall was built in northern England by Roman Emperor Hadrian to keep tribal Pics out of Scotland.

2 Aborigine Wall Art

Aborigines display the world's oldest continuous tradition of visual art on the numerous cliff and cave walls throughout Australia. Each year, at the end of the dry season, some paintings are restored by retracing the outlines of animals. Aborigines believe this ensures the multiplication of species and a good hunting season.

The Aborigines' ancestors were the first people to live in Australia. Today Aborigines would like to win government recognition for their land titles, achieve social equality, preserve their identity and heritage, and elect more legislators to the Australian parliament.

3 The Lascaux Cave

This cave was opened to visitors, limited to five hundred a day, in 1945. By 1960 a green mold caused by human breath had covered many of the paintings and the cave was closed to the public. Paintings on rock walls can be seen in many countries including Canada, Spain, Turkey, Zimbabwe, Egypt, India and Korea.

4 The Western Wall

Jerusalem is the holy city of three major religious groups–Jews, Christians, and Muslims. The Old City of Jerusalem, which is built where ancient Jerusalem used to be, is enclosed by walls. Inside is the Western Wall, the holiest site in the world for Jews. Traditionally, Jewish women have only prayed alone at the wall, while men have been allowed to pray alone or in groups. Since 1988, many Jewish women have been challenging the inequality of this custom by praying in groups at the wall.

Built in 961 B.C., the 59-foot-high wall is a portion of the western retaining wall of Temple Mount, one of Islam's greatest shrines. Also located nearby is the Church of the Holy Sepulchre, believed to be built over the site of Jesus' crucifixion.

Today, people of at least twenty-one different sects live in Jerusalem, a city governed by the Israelis. There is frequent turmoil, conflict, and tension as these different people struggle for what they believe is theirs.

On November 9, 1989, thousands of jubilant Germans went to a street party at the Berlin Wall. Their cheers, cries, and songs could be heard for miles as East and West Germans who had been kept apart for more than twenty-five years came together to tear down the wall.

The Berlin Wall, constructed in 1961, became a physical part of an invisible barrier that had divided Eastern and Western Europe since 1945. At that time Winston Churchill, the leader of Great Britain, called this invisible barrier the "Iron Curtain" because he believed the Soviet Union wanted to divide countries and take them over. Joseph Stalin, the leader of the Soviet Union at that time, thought this invisible wall would protect his country from further invasion.

Many people living in Europe grew weary of the walls that separated them from their neighbors. For years these people dreamed of the day when their voices of protest would lift the Iron Curtain and their hands would tear down the Berlin Wall. People throughout the world were amazed when the Berlin Wall finally did come down in 1989. Since then the borders of many Eastern European countries have opened, reuniting friends and families and neighbors.

Nelson Mandela spent twenty-six birthdays within hostile South African prison walls. The thousands of birthday cards sent to him might have brightened his bleak walls, but prison officials never allowed Mandela to read them.

The majority of the people in South Africa are black, yet for many generations they had no say in how their government was ruled. Since Mandela was a young man, he has spoken out for freedom and fairness for all South Africans. The people in the white-ruled government were scared of Mandela's ideas of justice and in 1964 sentenced him to life in jail.

Many people were angry that Mandela was jailed. For years they marched and chanted "Free Nelson Mandela." This song of protest rang out around the world. As a result of these protests, Nelson Mandela was freed from his prison walls on February 11, 1990 and four years later he was elected President of South Africa. During this election in April, 1994, Mandela and millions of black South Africans cast the first votes of their lives.

Today Mandela continues to talk about freedom. He says that all the people of South Africa must unite and work together.

Flowers, letters, candles, and boots are lovingly placed under the names written on the Vietnam Veterans Memorial, in Washington, D.C. Each day these mementos and many others are left at the long, black reflective wall that rises out of the earth. The monument is about one hundred sixty-five giant steps long and was designed by Maya Lin, a twenty-one-year-old architecture student. She chose black granite for her design because she felt you could gaze into it forever. Every day people come to visit the wall, and many cry as they look at, touch, and remember the names of American men and women who were killed or are still missing as a result of the war in Vietnam.

Many more men, women, and children died during this war. If the names of these Vietnamese, Cambodian, and Laotian dead were chiseled into the wall, it would extend for at least another seven thousand giant steps.

The limestone walls of the Canadian Museum of Civilization in Hull, Quebèc, across the river from Ottawa, resemble the melting glaciers and windswept rocks of the Western Canadian Shield. Douglas Cardinal, an architect from Alberta, feels such respect for his homeland that he designed the exterior walls of this museum to look like the landforms of Canada.

The museum displays encourage visitors to wander through thousands of years of Canadian history. Many exhibits also celebrate the creative genius of all people by showing that the world is truly a global village. Children can dress up in international costumes, play in an igloo, and listen to street scenes from around the world aboard a colorfully decorated bus. On their way in and out of the museum, visitors marvel at the splendid totem poles that were carved by the first people of western Canada.

The walls that Diego Rivera painted are like the pages of a large picture book. Many of the huge murals that he painted on walls throughout Mexico show the glorious and painful history of his country. Women hard at work with babies on their backs, farmers bending over in the fields, and people fighting for their rights are just some of the characters that Rivera portrayed in his murals.

An artist of tremendous energy and passion, Rivera worked for ten, twelve, sometimes fourteen hours a day. He painted to share his vision of Mexico's history with his people.

Every day for more than eight hundred years, the children of Taos pueblo in New Mexico have climbed up and down ladders that lead into their five-story homes. This sunbaked adobe compound continues to be the home of the Pueblo people because no one has succeeded in pushing them off their lands, though many have tried. The residents of the Taos pueblo are proud that they live comfortably within the walls that their people have occupied for more than thirty generations.

Visitors are welcome to watch the traditional Deer and Turtle dances at the pueblo, yet no one but the pueblo people are allowed inside the walls of the ceremonial kivas. This is one of the ways in which the people of Taos pueblo preserve the sacred, private aspects of their culture.

In June, Incas gather for a celebration at their walls in Cuzco, Peru, a city that lies high in the Andes Mountains. Many of the stones that were used long ago to build these walls are three and four times taller than a grown person. It is hard to imagine how such enormous stones could have been moved without modern tools, so people have made up stories to explain how the walls were built. Some say that supernatural beings built the Cuzco walls; others claim that the ancient Incan masons knew how to change stone into liquid.

Today at these walls, Incas celebrate the festival of Inti Rayma. They sit on the gigantic fortress walls that were built by their ancestors more than six hundred years ago. Here they listen to the haunting sounds of ancient instruments and watch traditional dances that honor the sun.

Many mysteries used to surround the ancient gray-green granite walls of Great Zimbabwe in southeast Africa. Who built the stately circular walls that were home to the thousands of Shona people more than a thousand years ago? Why did the Shona abandon this once noble city after they had lived there so many years? What was the purpose of the conical tower built within the walls?

Today people know that it was not builders from other places but the ancestors of the skilled Shona masons who carefully hand cut, trimmed, and piled stones one by one to build Great Zimbabwe. In the Shona language, *Zimbabwe* means "stone enclosure."

The Shona moved away from Great Zimbabwe, once a busy trade center, because many of the area's natural resources had been depleted. Still unsolved is the mystery of why the masons built the tower. Some think it was a sacred place. Others think it was used for storage. No one really knows.

The paintings on the outside walls of this Egyptian house tell a story about a very personal journey. It is the story of a pilgrimage from this village to the southwestern Saudi Arabian city of Mecca, the holiest place in the Islamic world.

As children, many Muslims learn that one day they will be asked to make a trip to Mecca where Muhammad, the founder of their religion, was born. Every year millions of Muslims speaking hundreds of different languages travel to Mecca to perform seven rituals. First, while they pray, they walk or run around the Ka'aba, a shrine whose walls protect a sacred stone. After the pilgrims complete six other rituals, they return home from Mecca and are then called *Hadjiis*. The decorated walls are a proud reminder of their pilgrimage.

Crafty cats, proud bulls, enormous elephants, and curious monkeys are a few of the many larger-than-life animals that have been carved into the cliffs near India's Bay of Bengal.

In Hindu myths and Indian tales, many of these animals think and talk like humans. Elephants bring rain and good luck in the myths, and the tales tell how clever monkeys outwit scheming crocodiles.

The sounds of chisels and hammers could be heard in India almost two thousand years ago as artists crafted the splendid animals on the rock walls. Today the sounds of children's voices can be heard as they play near these majestic Indian animals.

From before the sun comes up until long after bedtime, Jewish children and their families come to tuck special pieces of paper in the ancient Western Wall in Jerusalem. Solemnly they place their handwritten Hebrew prayers in the wall's worn crevices.

Every day crowds of worshippers from all over the world gather at the towering structure that was once the western wall of King Solomon's temple. It is often called the Wailing Wall because many Jewish people lament that their temple was destroyed more than two thousand years ago. One of their prayers is that it will be rebuilt one day.

Searching for their dog in the thick brambles of the French woods in 1940, four boys found a small hole in the ground. After digging and shimmying through the narrow hole, they discovered an abandoned cave. Their curiosity led them to explore its dark interior. Once inside they were amazed to see tumbling horses, charging bison, and leaping antelope magnificently painted on the walls of this Lascaux cave.

After keeping the treasured cave secret for several days, the boys finally shared their find with a trusted teacher. They soon learned that the wall paintings were created more than seventeen thousand years ago. The people who drew these pictures didn't cook, sleep, or play in this cave or any of the other caves in the area. The caves were used only for special hunting and religious ceremonies.

When this Aborigine boy was eight years old, he placed his hand next to his father's handprint and spread apart his small brown fingers. Then he blew a chalky white powder between his fingers onto the wall. He is very proud to return and find his handprint on the rock wall.

This rock wall and many others like it in Australia are covered with handprints and a collection of figures: skeletal fish, darting kangaroos, and people on horseback. Aborigines, descendants of Australia's first people, read their history in these paintings, some of which are more than thirty thousand years old.

Many paintings tell stories of the Aborigines' love of the land and of how they and their ancestors have always taken good care of the earth. Other, more recent paintings, tell of a terrible time when settlers came by ship with guns and took the land away from them. Today Aborigines continue to tell their stories with wall and tree-bark paintings.

According to an old tale, the only structure on earth that can be seen from the moon is the magnificent Great Wall of China. For about fifteen hundred miles this ancient fortress twists and turns like a massive stone serpent across the mountains, plains, and deserts of China. Chinese children and their families and people from many other countries love to visit the wall where they walk along a path, as wide as five horses, that winds along the top of the wall.

More than two thousand years ago, large stones and granite boulders were used to construct much of the wall's eastern side. Bricks that were formed by pounding together moistened dirt made up sections of the western side. Some say the Great Wall was built to keep out invaders. Others say it was built to keep the Chinese at home.

Talking Walls

Margy Burns Knight

Illustrated by Anne Sibley O'Brien

Tilbury House, Publishers

Before I built a wall I'd ask to know
What I was walling in or walling out. . .

Robert Frost

To Kyle and Emilie and to Perry and Yunhee

All over the world, every hour of the day, there are
people of all ages, races, and creeds working hard to create
a world without walls that hurt people.
We dedicate this book to them.

Margy Burns Knight and Anne Sibley O'Brien

Tilbury House, Publishers
03 Brunswick Avenue, Gardiner, ME 04345
00–582–1899 • www.tilburyhouse.com

14 13 12 11 10

brary of Congress Cataloging-in-Publication Data
night, Margy Burns.
    Talking walls / Margy Burns Knight : illustrated by
Anne Sibley O'Brien.
        p. cm.
    Summary: An illustrated description of walls around
he world and their significance, from the Great Wall of
China to the Berlin Wall.
    ISBN 0-88448-102-6. -- ISBN 978-0-88448-154-6 (pbk)
    1. Walls--Juvenile literature. [1. Walls. 2. World
istory.]
. O'Brien, Anne Sibley, ill. II. Title.
TH2201.K64 1992
00--dc20   91-67867
                        CIP
                        AC

ext designed on Crummett Mountain by Edith Allard
iting and production: Mark Melnicove
iting and production assistance: Liz Pierson, Devon
illips, Dianne Webb Payne
agesetting: High Resolutions, Inc., Camden, Maine
lor Separations: Graphic Color Service, Fairfield, Maine
nted and bound at Worzalla, February 2010,
35 Jefferson Sreet, Stevens Point, WI 54481

knowledgements:
cerpt from *Poems and Sketches of E.B. White*. Copyright
33 by E.B. White. Reprinted by permission of
arperCollins Publishers.
cerpt from "Mending Wall" by Robert Frost from *The
try of Robert Frost*, Henry Holt and Company, Inc.

kotel

UKUTA

CIDAR

MURO

People all over the world have been using and building walls for thousands of years. These walls tell many fascinating stories.

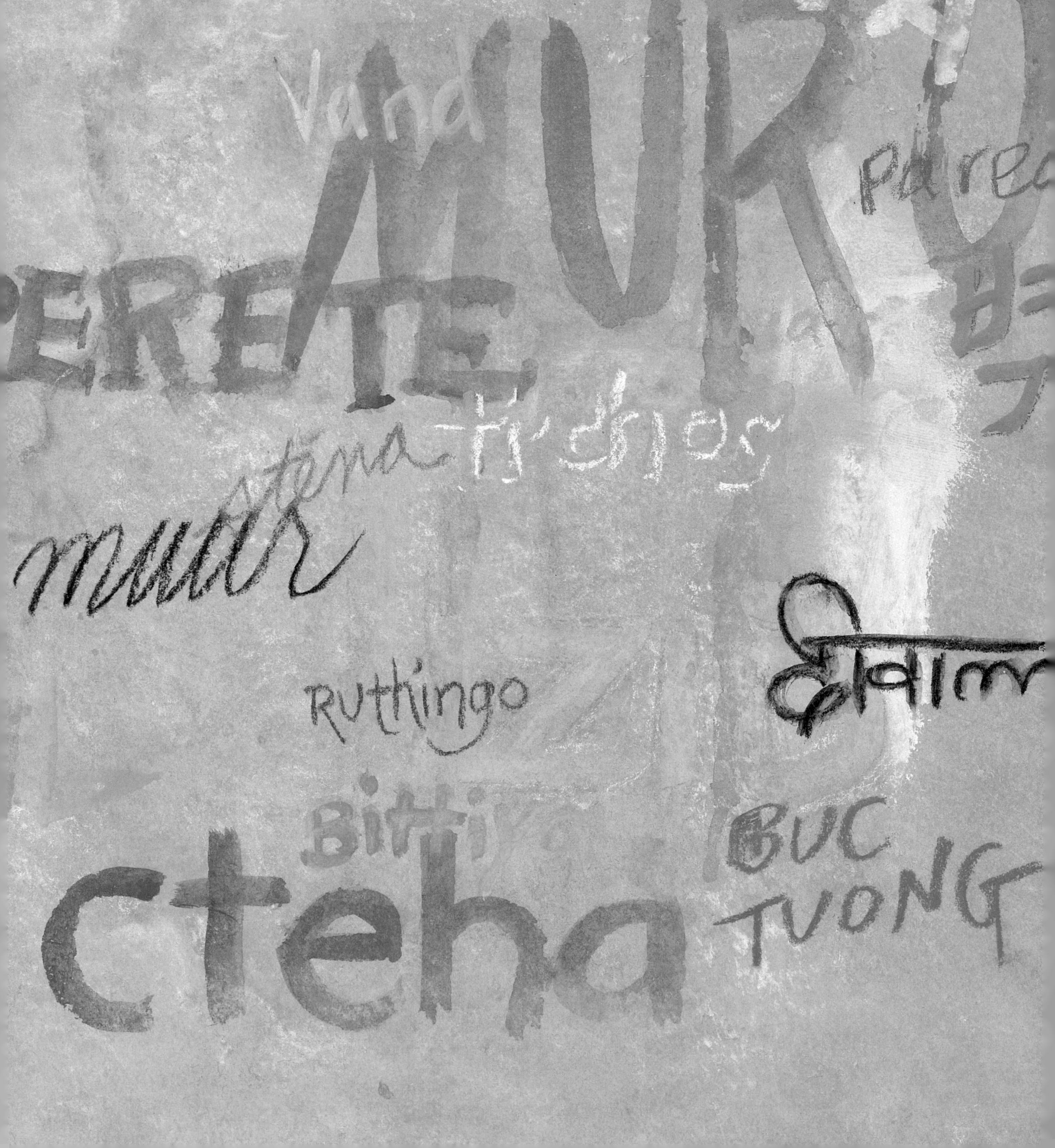

Vand

pared

PERETE

stena ti dros

mutr

दीवाल

ruthingo

Bitti

cteha

BUC TUONG

7706

7706